Also from Sixteen Rivers Press

Snake at the Wrist, by Margaret Kaufman
Translations from the Human Language, by Terry Ehret
difficult news, by Valerie Berry

After Cocteau

After Cocteau

CAROLYN MILLER

SIXTEEN RIVERS PRESS

Printed in the United States of America

My thanks to the following publications,
in which some of the poems in this book first appeared:

A Small Box of Poets (Protean Press), *Aunties* (Wildcat Canyon Press), *Barnabe Mountain Review, Centering, The Chattahoochee Review, Constant Lover* (Protean Press), *Cumberland Poetry Review, The Georgia Review, Kansas Quarterly/Arkansas Review, Maryland Poetry Review, New York Quarterly, Nobody's Child* (Baywood Publishing), *Painted Hills Review, Poets On: Forgetting, Quarterly West, Seattle Review, Shenandoah, Southern Poetry Review, The Southern Review, VIVO, Where the Heart Is* (Wildcat Canyon Press), *Whispering Campaign, Wilderness, Yellow Silk, Zone 3*, and *ZYZZYVA*

Special thanks to the Koret Foundation
for their support of Sixteen Rivers Press

Published by Sixteen Rivers Press
P.O. Box 640663
San Francisco, CA 94164-0663
www.sixteenrivers.com

Library of Congress Catalog Card Number: 2001-126716
ISBN 0-9707370-3-3

Cover art: *Night Ocean,* 1995, Carolyn Miller,
acrylic on paper mounted on canvas

For Tom McAfee

The soul striving to attain the divine state by its own efforts falls into total despair, and suddenly there dawns upon it with a great illuminative shock the realization that the divine state simply is, here and now, and does not have to be attained.

—Alan Watts

Contents

Part Three

PART ONE

Simple Mysteries

Lupine, for example: its dry
Mediterranean clinging to the hills, its gray-green
furry pods, its beaked flowers like
a woman's genitals—the wide banners and small wings
and the closed, smooth keel—the love of bees
for it, the private smell of lupine flesh, the fishlike
glimmer of its yellow heart, the deep blue
blossoms strung on stems above
the blue-gray palmate leaves
like flocks of small, intensely colored birds
blurring the hillsides into fields of blue, the world
broken into flower
without our even asking.

After Cocteau: Beauty's Father in the Castle of the Beast

for Lee Hildreth

When the thorny hedge opened for him,
he was astonished; when it closed
behind him, the leaves and twigs
knitting themselves seamlessly together
in the darkness, fear
flooded his body, and went with him
on the path through the wild garden,
up the steps of the mist-veiled castle.
Then the massive door opened without a touch,
and he saw, in the long, stony hall, a row of human arms
holding lighted candelabras.
Yet when the white arms moved, each in turn,
to light his way, he did not go back.
No, he had not imagined it; and although
he hesitated, something compelled him forward,
and he walked on until he came
into a vaulted room, where it seemed clear
that he had been expected: the fire leaping
behind the andirons, the candles lighted,
a table set for one, laden with food and wine.
And somehow it hardly seemed surprising
that parts of this room were alive:
When the eyes in the faces carved into the mantel
moved to watch him, he did not leave;
instead he felt his fear mix with desire

for warmth and food, and so he simply sat down
at the table. Even when a living hand
reached to fill his glass with wine
and lift the cover from the steaming roast,
his appetite grew larger than his fear,
and he ate as if he belonged
in that circle of light, as if he were a prince
and the feast his due.
When he had eaten and drunk his fill
from the bowls that did not empty
and the jug of wine that did not diminish,
he was so suffused with satisfaction that,
despite himself, sleep came over him
in that alien place, even though
the lion's head carved into the armrest
beneath his hand opened its mouth and roared.
And so, a stranger and alone, he fell asleep,
having accepted all he knew so far of the story:
the thorns, the dark path, the gifts, the magic.

Meditations on the Ascension

What did Jesus think
when he finally was released?
Out of the choking tomb
and done at last
with appearing and disappearing,
showing up out of nowhere,
touching down,
making little clouds of dust
with his mangled feet,
holding out his hands
full of holes.
And when he left the world,
I wonder if he took off
lying on his back, arms
folded on his chest, or if
he just shot slowly up
like a ball from a Roman candle,
making a soft *thocking* sound?

It might almost be worth it
to be the sacrificial lamb,
to rise up, to be let go
from the painful wheel of time,
to be pried off the material cross,
to look down and see the earth
like a blue and green marble
bobbling along in space.

Though I love the earth,
with its runny fluids,
its sponge and bone, its flux
and absolutes, I might give it up
to ascend quietly through layers
of color and density, ozone
and oxygen, old birthday balloons
and lost kites, floating
constantly upward through
the ions and electrons,
passing eventually into the blackness
of space, beyond gas molecules
and memory, like a fish
in an ocean canyon,
settling in for the duration,
patiently maintaining my thrust,
humming steadily along, waiting
to emerge from the terrible cold
into the blinding realm.

Yet I wonder if Jesus is torn
in his heart, as his flesh
was ripped in his side?
Does he miss the certainty of decay,
the hard facts of death
and rot? Does he miss
the clamor of the crowd,

the changing spotlight of the sun?
Sitting up there on God's right hand
for eternity, the air packed full
of angels jostling
and elbowing one another, poking
with their wing tips,
the constant, maddening rustling
of feathers, the whir
and the furling
and unfurling of wings,
lined up according to class
like chickens on a roost,
the streets shining relentlessly,
such a bright yellow.

A Dream of Flying: The Amelia Earhart Story

Amelia Earhart learned to fly
against the wishes of her parents.

—The Encyclopedia Britannica

I will, I will! she said,
flapping her arms for practice under the covers,
with a great stirring of sheets
and a slumping of quilts.
Often, after dark, she would crawl
from her bedroom window where it opened out
onto the asbestos-shingled roof,
walking on all fours up the angle between the peaks
to lie on the slanted back roof of the house in her nightgown,
looking up at the stars, yearning to lift
toward the speckled firmament.
Later she slept coiled in her bedclothes
like an angel in white robes unable to rise.
Sometimes she would run as fast as she could possibly run;
sometimes she would go too fast over the blacktop
on her metal skates; and sometimes she raced
downhill out of control on her Flexible Flyer,
hoping against all reason that this time
she would slowly begin to rise, gravity letting go
of her reluctantly like the frightened hands of her parents.
She jumped from heights again and again—
the garden shed, the fenced-in back porch,
the second-floor balcony—landing time after time
on her shocked, hurt feet, as though the earth

were punishing her for wanting to leave. She sat long hours
in the scratchy arms of trees. She watched the ends
of her fingers, looking for pinions; she felt the two
V-shaped bones on her back, hoping for shafts of feathers
to sprout from her skin. She dreamed of flying,
of a high, clean place where she would be completely free,
of looking down on clouds, only the moon
and the stars above her, of seeing the continents
and glinting oceans laid out like puzzle pieces, of passing over
the Himalayas and Alps, their white peaks close enough
to touch. She dreamed of cold, thin air rushing over
her body as she arrowed through the atmosphere,
of consorting with birds, of racing with eagles,
of seeing far below, through the haze,
her fearful, earthbound parents
craning their necks toward heaven,
hoping in vain for her return.

Summer Sonnet

The lovers rise around me in the air;
their twining arms lift up like butterflies
or cyclamen. The colors of their eyes
are bluet, iris, columbine. Their hair
is streaming back; their long white feet are bare,
like the feet of saints. The sharp blue skies
encircle them, for they are held by ties
of jealous earth and time. How unaware,
how beautiful they are! I reach my hand
to touch them, but our bodies cannot meet.
They do not see me watching, still alone
in summertime, among the leaves. I stand
far below them on the shimmering street.
Life is skipping past me like a stone.

The Reluctant Dinner Guest

I sat at the table of life. Then he
walked by and saw me sitting there
alone. He joined me, by impulse,
I suppose. I was pleased, for I had long
hoped to feast with him. *Here,*
I said, *fried chicken, glistening*
outside, juicy in. I fed him
the white meat with my hands. Great
rounded mounds of mashed potatoes, rich
with butter and heavy cream. Smooth
pan gravy to pool on top, tender spears
of new asparagus. Crisp, tart watercress
and firm, vine-ripe tomatoes, coated with
wine vinegar and virgin olive oil.
And afterward, dense lemon pie, topped with
a cloud of pale meringue.

He seemed satisfied enough with my food.
And there is no denying he was hungry—
he ate so fast. Almost before the meal
was through, he pushed back his chair
to go. I was sad to see him leave,
for I had thought that he might tarry
at the table, taking just one more hot
biscuit, one more slice of pie.

For a time I sat there, food
cooling around me, crusts and skins
forming on its surfaces, islands of fat
solidifying on the sauces.
Then one day he wandered by again
and seemed surprised to see me there.
I offered him some of my specialties:
plump pillows of *gnocchi verde,*
risotto milanese, billowy
warm foam of *zabaglione*.

Well, he didn't know. He had so
many other things to do. I said, *Would you like*
raw oysters, tasting of the sea,
slipping down your throat? Oozing
Camembert and Brie? Or prosciutto e melone,
the pink translucent ham
wrapped around chilled sweet cantaloupe?
Porc braisé aux choux rouges?
Or lamb chops, thick ones,
rare inside, rubbed with
broken garlic cloves? Fat
heavy loaves of country bread
with fresh curls of sweating butter and,
at the end, reine de saba,
studded with coarse-crushed almonds,
slicked with a semisweet chocolate glacé?

Then he explained he didn't really *like*
full-course meals. It wasn't that
he wasn't hungry—he just preferred to eat
and run, grazing at different tables. But,
he said, as long as he was here,
he might have a nibble, just a bite
or two.

Still, I tried to tempt him with dessert,
offering him many cunning
forms of *dolci:* chewy *amaretti,*
dead-ripe black figs napped with
double cream, *gelati* rough with hazelnuts,
and bright *sorbetti* clogged with fruit.
Hard little bites of chocolate truffles
with espresso, dark, silky chocolate mousse
to melt on his tongue, tiny glasses of
intense liqueurs. I promised him
that if he'd stay the night,
for breakfast I would give him *cappuccini,*
warm *briosce* with raspberry jam,
or scones with mountain honey and clotted
cream, orange juice just squeezed,
late peaches, heaping bowls
of summer berries with *crème fraîche*. But no,
he said, he had to go.

After that, he dropped by
from time to time, and now and then
he seemed inclined to dally.
There were evenings when a steaming entrée
seemed to hold him—particularly,
as I recall, my *chiles rellenos*.
And I remember clearly how he lingered
over my *huevos rancheros* with *salsa fresca,*
not to mention the quivering flan,
warm caramel running down its sides. And
all that time, his presence alone
was food to me: his hair the color of wheat,
his smell of bitter fruit. Then
it was enough to have him seated at my table.
But finally my hunger grew for more.

The table of life is long and wide,
but life itself is short.
I have learned that it is better to dine alone
than to share your food
with a reluctant guest. And even now,
I know, somewhere outside my windows
future guests are passing.
Today, I threw away
his spotted place card and the withered
centerpiece, changed the linens,

polished up my pots. I'm ready for
someone with a strong, enduring
appetite, someone who'll stay long
at the table, who'll reach out
and fill my plate, saying:
Bagna cauda? Pasta con funghi? Scampi
ai spiedi? Someone who'll pour out
plummy Pinot Noir or steely Chardonnay
or clear, cold Fumé Blanc until my glass
flows over. Who'll say, *Do you want*
some more? until we fill each other with
a sweet, deep nourishment.

At the End of Summer

All day I have been tired from making love to you,
the muscles in my neck, my inner thighs,
my buttocks, strained and tight. A quiet day,
late September. Home alone, I think about you
off and on throughout the day,
how a dark cloud of hair begins at your breastbone,
your small nipples hidden in it. How it grows
thickly across your torso, down your stomach
to your genitals.

I left you at midnight and walked home.
High above me, a mass of warm moist air from Mexico
was colliding with the cold Pacific air.
At three o'clock a great electrical storm,
like a storm out of my childhood, ignited
in the sky. I stood on my back porch a long time,
listening to the rain and thunder,
watching the lightning branch and burn as if
the sky would break wide open.

The year is moving into autumn; the equinox
is only days away. Weeks ago
people began to say, *Well, fall is almost here.*
The mornings have turned darker; both at morning
and at night there is a coldness in the air.

I liked looking at you in the light,
a tall, beautiful man, your long legs,
your large hands, the small cave of your navel,
both of us slick with sweat like water mammals,
our hair wet at the roots. You talked to me
as we made love, unhurried.
The world is large, and it is lovely
to be kind to one another.
Outside, the air is cool, shadowed,
as if the day had a secret. You swim
in and out of my mind from time to time,
like making love,
then resting from making love.

What It Was Like There

We lived in an old house in San Francisco, three of us,
in the lower flat; a little family living in the high
shadowy rooms. It was a melancholy house, belonging,
like all our houses, to someone else. A century was trapped
in its wood and bumpy plaster. Everything trembled,
the windows rattling nervously in their tracks,
each time a bus went by. In winter the cold moved in with us,
sinking into the dishes, the furniture, our bones.
Year-round, the odor of mildew rose from black blossoms
growing on the walls. My children and I passed each other warily,
hoping nothing would be asked of us. In the kitchen,
the old cat, stunned by time, tightened into a ball.
I sat, surrounded by all the things I hadn't done, surprised
by my life. In my bedroom with its peeling deep-rose paint:
the smell of human flesh, thick as the smell of ripened fruit.

From our front windows we could see the bay
through little amputated sycamores. In summer, rivers of fog
flowed past us over the water; tourists in bright clothes
moved up and down the street in the ocean wind.
A silly place, but beautiful beyond shame, the bay
sinking and welling under the sky, the water and the air
never the same two days in a row—the bay sheeted with light,
fused with a silver sky; or both dissolving in one dying blue,
neither only water or only air; or the water the intense
blue-green of a photograph, or with an opaque smoke-blue mist

rising from it in one dense layer, or sullen,
a dead gray, having swallowed the light; or its vast body
turned the pale, unearthly color of an opal, lighted
from within—so that at last I realized
our lives were passing in that place, filled with a beauty
I could not understand.

Looking Out My Kitchen Window in Late June

In my garden, new flies spiral in the sun
like small white parachutes against the thick
dark vines. The orange trumpet flowers spill over
and over the wall. The house is still.
The kitchen smells of peaches. Outside: summer,
swelling like a wave. For a moment,
there is nothing that I want.

Robinson Grown Old

The old cat is now impossibly old.
For almost twenty years she has clicked her way
across my floors to hunker down,
narrowing her eyes at life, collapsing
slowly into sleep, her eyeballs
rolling back sideways.

Most of that time she was solid, gleaming,
a gray and black tabby cat, fat
and bristling as a bumblebee. Always
I admired her perfect symmetrical stripes,
her apricot belly, her broad
unintelligent face, every orifice delicately
bordered with a fine black line.
Completely pleased with herself,
with her flashy black leg bands and
the bold brush strokes on her sides,
she spent years dozing among the pillows,
humming like a small bagpipe under the fern.
And when I held her, her happiness grew
so large, it fluttered in her throat
like a swallowed bird.

But she changed; she began to grow thinner,
reminding me more and more of Edith Piaf,
down to the crooked eyeliner and desperate croak.
For a little while this was funny;
having lost control of her legs, she toppled about,
lurching through doorways as though
electrically charged,
all her pretty pussyfooting gone.
Sort of a bag lady of a cat, in her ratty
old fur coat too big for her bones,
she grew lighter and lighter until
her amusement value disappeared.
Now she is little more than clouded eyes
and a large throb. Incontinent,
she is banished to the back of the house;
the sour smell of her pee hangs in my rooms.
She hunches on the floor as if she were cold,
making a harsh, uneven noise
like a broken accordion. In sleep
she falls forward on her face
like a drunk passed out in a bar. Sometimes,
beyond all distinctions,
she naps in her cat pan and voids in her bed,
so I have to bathe her, terrified
that she will shrink to nothing.

In the slightly crossed black moons of her eyes,
she is asking for something I cannot give.
She teeters across the floor
as if it were the narrow limb of a tree,
and sits for hours on the back stairs
in the dark, somewhere between
the world of sound
and the world of silence.

Picking Blackberries, Stinson Beach

Late September. Only a few people at the beach, and the road is lined with ripe blackberries. When my young daughters and I walk into the bushes in our shorts and sandals, tiny red marks, like cat scratches, spring to the surface of our skin. The berries shine like animal eyes among the fat green leaves, and the branches droop almost to the ground with great handfuls of heavy fruit—so many berries, we are amazed—all within reach, as though they were being held out to us; fully ripe, with no red pockets of sourness, and only a few musky with decay or bitter with insect stings—and we realize that we have found an earthly blackberry heaven.

We eat all the biggest ones—great ovals, swollen and complete as little jars, or lanterns—but almost at once, it seems, our newspaper cones are packed with the dense bodies of berries, and deep-red juice pools in the bottom. The bright green, almost translucent hooks on the silvery canes catch at our clothes and try to hold us, but we pull free, fine bramble hairs sprouting from our hands and feet. Small fountains of blood crust on our legs, and, looking up at one another, we see that our hands and faces are stained with crimson, as if we were warriors at the end of a fierce battle.

At home, I cook the berries into a pie, leaving smears of red on the counter and pastry board. The sugar draws even more juice from the glossy sacs; in the uncooked pie, berries sink in a purple sea. In the oven, liquid spurts from the crust to form miniature volcanoes; lava flows over the edges and onto the oven floor, where it caramelizes into foamy mountains and blackens to cinders, sending out an acrid, burnt-sugar smell.

Now the pie, browned and spattered, has cooled on the back porch, but the kitchen is still warm, and filled with the odor of cooked fruit. Already, this blackberry pie has passed into legend. When I cut it open, it pours out a juice as dark and rich as dragon's blood.

Riding the 30 Stockton

Outside the bus the world sinks deeper:
So far two days and a night of solid rain,
and tonight the streets fill with dark paint;
the houses and buildings groan
like swimmers reluctant to enter the sea.
The windows of the bus run black
and silver. In the white fluorescent light
each damp face in the rows of faces is fleshy,
thickened. Inside my grocery bag a loaf
of sweet French bread is sending up
such small fat clouds of scent
I close my eyes with joy.

Department of Public Works

They're painting the Stockton Tunnel white. I wonder:
Why don't they paint it red, so that going into it
would be like entering the birth canal, or spurting through
an artery on a bright, salty stream? Or why not
paint it yellow, so that being inside would be like
falling into the sun; or orange, which would be like sinking
into the reflected fire of the sunset, or the center of
a tangerine, where you could die from the shocking
sweetness? If they painted it blue, driving through
would be like descending into the upper levels of the sea
just before the water darkens, or realizing at last
the dream of flying—just raise your arms and go up,
the way we always knew we could. Green would be
like passing through the rich stem of a plant,
its cells unlocking around you the moment before your body
unfolds into flower, and purple would be like slipping down
the inside of a morning glory, toward the narrow tube,
past the sticky stamen. And if it were black,
we could be seeds waiting under the soil; it would be
like night and death, and giving up memory and desire.

But no, they are painting it white, and for a few hours
passing through will be like imagining eternity, or
the stillness inside the avalanche—until it becomes,
once more, a tunnel that takes you from Sacramento to Sutter,
an exercise in loving the world as it is: urine streaked,
stained with rust, written on with Magic Marker, reading
MEAT IS MURDER, FUR IS FASCIST, FUCK THE QUEEN.

Still Life with Tropical Flowers

But it is not still: The flame claws of
the heliconia dangle from a bent neck
of stem, the scarlet wings of its fish spine
slicing the air; the bird-of-paradise
has flown here from an armored, dangerous Eden,
its reptilian head as alien as the helmet of
a samurai, its dagger beak opening to show
stiff orange standards, tiny lavender pikes.
The shiny red plastic heart
of the anthurium flaunts an erect, barbed
organ; the protea's shattered edges are
orange crystals growing toward the sun. Even the air
around these hard, hostile flowers seems startled
by the strangeness of the world.

PART TWO

Winter in California

How do the roses know what to do?
Without frost, without snow, they are born
effortlessly, like clusters of suns
in the empty little backyards. Back home
it's a terrible winter: The snow
hasn't been off the ground since Christmas;
farmers are struggling to reach their stock;
the deer and wild turkeys go hungry.
I remember the faint
winter sun, how lost and far away
it seemed, like a dream of the sun—
the clicking of sleet on dead leaves,
the bitter days smelling of metal—
while here the roses are blooming
like fools, and the hills slowly grow
a deep, luminous green.

Yet I remember
even in Missouri,
short sticky leaves of new grass,
green as paint,
just as unreal,
alive as fur under the brown
mat of the old grass,
long before you'd expect it.

Meeting in Late August

My mother always knew they were there,
blinding white, radiant with power.
As she cuts the enormous dahlias
with a kitchen knife, she is not surprised
to see the angel, glowing, with a sword of fire,
appear before her in the Missouri hills.

Aunt Daisy

After you were gone I realized that you were precious,
that in the world of aunts I would not have another,
and especially not a Daisy, who so loved me,
that I would not hear a boatlike car turn in on the gravel
of the driveway, and see you smiling, heavy and plain
in your flowered dress, or hear your wavering voice
tell about the days when the aunts and uncles were young,
and I understood that in the great, grand scheme of things,
of galaxies and molecules and the vast, expanding universe,
something irreplaceable had gone out of my life,
and not dreams, and not the spirit, and not the future world
would bring you back as you were again.

The Missouri Woods

First, they tried to keep me out, erecting thick
green barriers of brush, locking together
their rough leaves and slippery branches.
Saplings sprang back to lash me like little whips;
the arms of trees and claws of thorns and bristly pods
like animal paws held me back, and
twisting vines and prickly brambles tried to stop me,
but I fought my way past the dense, leafy outer wall.

Then they tried to keep me in their hot, shaded stillness,
where everything seemed to be breathing together,
even the brittle leaves lying in drifts
beneath the trees, and the damp miniature tundras of moss,
the limestone caves and great outcroppings of rock,
the rough, mottled black and gray bark of the trees,
the mayapples and dogwood and violets lifting up
out of the strong, sweet bed of rot.

Then they tried to stay with me, leaving their mark in blood
and milky sap on my arms and legs, dusting my skin
with pollen and mold, staining my knees with green.
So I emerged, leaves in my hair, socks matted
with stickers and burrs, chiggers and ticks
in the folds of my skin, seeds in my pants cuffs,
wildness in my heart.

Brush

Those historical society people just won't
leave me alone, says my mother. *Why,*
they're all just radicals! They want it all,
not just the butter cooling in the springhouse,
the hot yeast biscuits in the cast-iron skillet,
but the pregnant hired girl, the babies dead
from scarlet fever, the bloody sheets,
Uncle Mack drunk and beating the horses.
My mother thinks they're crazy, these people
not content with their central heat, their fiberglass
drapes and their refrigerator rolls, who long instead
to know what it was like to be an awkward
black-browed girl who rode a horse from Cookville
into Bloodland. She wants to forget it all: the straw ticks;
the one pair of shoes polished white for summer,
black for winter; the schoolchildren with their
mustard sandwiches and head lice; the stink
of unwashed wool and bodies by the wood stove.
She wants the past to disappear;
she has spent her life trying to cut it back
like the brush struggling up the hill toward
the big aluminum-sided house where she lives now,
miles from the old river-bottom farm.
It thrives, the tough, twisted green growth
of scrub oak and sumac, persimmon and buckeye;
despite ice storms and fires and rocky soil,

despite webworms and drought,
down in the woods in the hot Missouri summer
it radiates heat, it grows like disease, it tries
to come back and blot out the view of the valley,
to devour the roses, to dig its long, dark roots
in the beds of cannas and dahlias
my mother has cultivated so carefully.

Daughter of the Ozarks

I was allowed to try to kill the bluejays,
first with my BB gun, later with
the .22. They perched up in the oak trees,
metallic blue bundles of aggravation,
with their absurd little flattop head combs.
They were the greasers of the Missouri woods,
waiting to dive-bomb my father's strawberry patch,
lobbing themselves like grenades down from the black oaks
to plunge their beaks in the fat, seeded hearts
of the Everbearings. Of course, I never killed one,
or anything else, so I settled
for shooting the .22 from my backyard high on the hill
down into the distant Roubidoux. Even that far away
I could see the water splash
moments after I pulled the trigger, felt
the shove of the gun butt on my bony shoulder,
smelled the oil from the rifle barrel, scattered
the empty cartridges in the dirt.
So summer passed. I was nine or ten. I think
my hair was long; I think that was the summer of
the brown cowboy shirt and the aqua jumper, when I could run
over gravel barefoot without wincing; when I realized
I was immune to poison ivy and poison oak;
when every Sunday after church, my mother and father sleeping
in their chairs, my dog and I disappeared into the woods
with a batch of Duncan Hines blueberry muffins and

The Boy Scout Handbook; when I found the secret valley
with ferns and waterfalls and islands,
and no one knew or cared that I was gone for hours
out in the sticky green tangle of the woods.

Depth

My mother sends me clippings in the mail.
Two people have drowned while cave diving
in Roubidoux Spring. The spring is famous,
I now learn, to divers, who come hundreds of miles
to explore its underwater cave. It seems
that all the time I was growing up, my ugly little town
was resting on a lake, the county courthouse
and the row of bars, the bitter little churches
and the sandstone-puzzle houses were floating
on an aquifer, and what I thought was solid,
landlocked earth was underlined with caves
and tunnels and a hidden sea, the spring
exploding from it like an upside-down
waterfall, and the old mottled bluffs were looking out
on what was just the surface of reality,
while below the world of piano lessons,
and schoolyard fights, and little girls telling me
I was bossy, and my father's anger and
my mother's sorrow, and the sidewalks cracked
by the roots of elms was a dark, interior world
of convoluted passageways through rock, water
caves, and rivers flowing underground
beneath my ignorant, summer-hardened feet.

Poem for My Childhood

I was lucky, I had rivers: the Big Piney,
the Little Piney, the Little Tavern, the Gasconade,
the Roubidoux. They ran into each other like veins,
and in between were creeks and branches
and springs that bubbled up
like some kind of joy out of the earth,
like joy or grief, or maybe they were the same.
And I had bluffs and caves and sinkholes, and
a dry gully that came alive with waterfalls
after a heavy rain. All of this time I was
dancing inside my body, and my body was part
of the body of the Missouri hills. I believed
in the spirits of the woods, and I lived
my life in a fervor, a fervor for leaves
and for the flowers that appeared unasked for
in the loose shale of the hillside.

That was when my big brother figured out how
to get to the swimming hole at the foot of our hill
by running the entire way, breaking his steep descent
by leaping onto outcroppings of rock
and grabbing onto certain small trees
and swinging around them to slow his speed.
It was everything I wanted then and more:
my running brother, the wild hillside, and
at the bottom, the luminous Roubidoux,
rich with secrets.

Food

When they told me my mother had taken a turn
for the worse, I called up the airline
and made a reservation to go home. Then
I went into my kitchen and made hot cocoa,
just like we made back in the old kitchen
in Missouri: first a paste of Hershey's cocoa
and sugar with a little milk, then more milk
until it was the right color of cocoa brown.
I drank it all at once, and I could feel
the hot, sweet liquid burning down my throat,
and I knew I was alive. I went to the store
and bought strawberries, lots of them, three boxes
of shining, taut new California strawberries
almost as big as plums, and I bought bread and asparagus
and new red potatoes, tiny ones like the kind
my father used to grow, and I went home and made
creamed asparagus and new potatoes, and strawberries
sprinkled with sugar so that a sticky red juice collected
in the bottom of the bowl. I ate and ate,
because I was alive, and because I had
an appetite, like my mother had when she loved food
and when she was too heavy, before
she began to waste away to nothing and couldn't eat
at all. I ate the creamed vegetables and too much bread,
and I thought about all the years my mother had cooked
for us, so much food, the creamed chicken with biscuits,

the potato salad, the pies, the tall cakes—honest, unadorned
dishes from the Betty Crocker cookbook and the red-
and-white Good Housekeeping book and the mysterious old
falling-apart green book with the yellow-brown pages.
And I thought about how my mother's food
had made me feel safe and loved and cared for,
and I kept on eating bread and vegetables, and then
I ate the strawberries, so many that for once
I had almost all the strawberries I wanted, red and
streaming in the bowl, sliced open to reveal
their shimmering flesh and their knot-shaped hearts.

Home

I went back to another country,
which was the country of my childhood.
The garage lights and the back porch lights
were on. But when I opened the aluminum
storm door, for the first time my mother
was not there. The air of the long-closed house
rushed out to meet me, thick
with the smell of home: Jergen's lotion,
old wood, yellowed books, long-ago Thanksgivings,
vanished Christmas trees, innumerable peach and cherry
pies and angel food cakes, black skillets full
of frying chicken. There was the wavy
linoleum, the mismatched furniture,
the inaccurate clocks, the baskets of
old photographs and packets of faded letters, years
jumbled together as though
all of the past had happened at once.

My mother's bed is empty; she lies in the nursing home,
with her useless right leg and useless right arm
and her slurred, thick voice.
It's late, and I make up the bed in my room with
its cherry bedroom set and its faded organdy curtains;
my daughter sleeps in the bedroom across the hall.
The next day she drives us in the rental car
to the county home. The corridors smell like urine

and fear; everywhere are people in wheelchairs,
lost and stunned. When I enter my mother's room
with its shrunken welcome balloons, she knows me,
but her eyes are sunk in her head, surrounded
by deep shadow. She talks about the farm
where she was a girl; she recites *I wandered lonely*
as a cloud, and *The little toy dog was covered with dust,*
but she can't remember the endings. When I help
to turn her in the bed, she is stiff and straight,
heavy as stone, like a carved Etruscan queen,
and I am surprised to find that her flesh is as soft
and as white as a child's. When I ask her if she wants me
to stay until she sleeps, she says, "Oh,
I want you to stay *forever.*"

June in Missouri. Down in the valley, they are
haying, rolling up great spirals of summer
at intervals on the valley floor. The air
is expansive, warm, and sweet. I feel
embraced by it, and by the wide, open rooms
of the house. At night, I fall asleep on top of the covers
in the dark room of my childhood.
In the middle of the night, my daughter appears
in the doorway; she is afraid. She hears noises
and thinks someone is in the house. She crawls
into my bed. Long after she falls asleep,

I lie there listening. I am afraid, too. Yet
no one is here but us. It's only the house,
settling, its timbers and joists creaking,
the plaster slowly crumbling, the old
foundation cracking, everything going back
to the red clay and the rocky soil.

Big Piney River

This is the river that flows
out of Eden, rife
with minnows, effluvia,
tadpoles, yesterday's
rain, old shoes, turtles.
This is the water
of immortality:
a river clogged
with lilies, lined
with snake grass and skunk
cabbage, sheened with oil.
This is the moon road,
the stream of longing, boundary
for stupefied cows, crawdad
palace, frog paradise,
bed of heat and odor,
rainbowed with dragonflies, stitched
with water striders, buzzed
with horseflies, mired
with cattails, furred
with scum. Bird
fountain, snake mother,
trash eater, hog wallow, boat
bearer, spring drinker,

cloud mirror, fish cradle, star
map, echo maker, always
leaving, always arriving, deep
as an artery, green
with mystery, spangled
in the sun.

PART THREE

Early March, the Fruit Trees Still in Bloom

In the long rectangle of my bedroom window, everything is blue:
six o'clock after a day of rain, Sunday; the sky a lighted
blue with smudgy clouds moving through it; blue-gray
wooden San Francisco houses, criss-crossed back stairs,
flat roofs and chimney pots; the window-well lined with pipes
and blistered paint. No other window in the world
has just this view.

At Green Gulch today, rain passed over the zendo
in waves, and a pinecone crashed onto the roof as we sat
in meditation; sitting next to the wood stove,
I could hear rain falling quietly into the chimney pipe.
Following my breath, I realized that each inhalation is
a decision to live. A Buddhist priest told us this story:
When students came to see Katagiri Roshi, to tell him
they were full of pain, or sorrow, or anger,
Katagiri Roshi would say to each one, regardless:
"It's the flower of your life force blooming,
isn't it?" and each one would go away comforted.

Outside my window, everything grows darker, bluer.
I can hear the muffled sounds of people talking, moving
in other apartments. I go down inside myself, past
my loneliness, to the place of unquestionable belonging.
This is the flower of my life force blooming, isn't it.

Driving in to Tassajara

Tassajara . . . the first Buddhist monastery
outside Asia . . . is in a very remote location,
with the sole access being a 14-mile dirt road
that is quite steep and rugged. Not all cars
can safely negotiate this road. . . .

—Tassajara brochure

Though he is dead, E. Power Biggs plays Bach
toccatas and fugues on my tape deck
as I drive on the dangerous road, trying not to die;
his white fingers gleam on white organ keys
in candlelight in a dank cathedral in Europe,
while my car slides sideways on gravel in California,
climbing past changing colors of white oak and maple.
It's so hard to know about danger, where it is
and how much, so hard to keep fear from crowding out joy,
beating mothlike somewhere outside me, even though
the small, moving space of my car spills over with
the music of joy, of the clear certitude
of belonging in life, while reaching up
into the world of spirit.

I crest on the part of the road where waves
of hills and mountains roll back to the horizon
as varied and layered as clouds—gray green, purple gray,
blue on blue, shimmering in September light—
and I am filled with the sudden sense
of being lost in the world, alone on the spine
of this inland range in the sun, on an empty
road of yellow rocks and dust; yet in the next moment
it comes to me that I am, after all, inseparable

from the live oaks twisting out of the ground,
the leathery leaves of tan oak and madrone, the stretches of
golden grass on the hillsides; I am
in the world, part of its body in life and in death.
The sound of the great pipe organ fills my car,
shaking and glorious. The music of clarity,
of ordered, infinite worlds, it rises over
time and sorrow, and Freiburg Cathedral
sails like a great masted ship on swells of sound
as I steer down the steep, tortuous grade,
pumping my brakes, willing myself to live.

Walking to the Narrows, I Remember My Friend Virginia

How she walked the twenty-minute path
    from Tassajara, her feet, like her hands, curled
with pain. It was July then, the days were
    hotter, a stronger smell of dust in
the air, a sense of the world holding its breath,
    the sunlight almost cruel. At tea today
a German woman said, *Oh, the light*
    is so different now. I was here in June and
it was so bright it was hard to see.
    But now the light has changed, and everything
is so much closer. In September
    I always think of Keats and the ode
"To Autumn," and how well he understood
    the heartbreaking beauty of his life.
Virginia did everything when we were here,
    walking to the Narrows, trying all
the yoga postures, getting up at 5 A.M.
    for the first zazen, happily placing her shoes
outside our Japanese-style cabin,
    reading from one of Basho's travel books.
Imagine what a wonderful place the world would be,
    she said, *if everyone would sit quietly just*
a few minutes every day. She was in her early seventies,
    worried that an old friend
in his nineties would die while she was away.

Now both are dead, and the path is empty
through the laurels and the live oaks
along the stream. Driving here,
I thought how van Gogh would have loved the live oaks,
charged, as they seem to be, with energy,
their dark angulations and tough hooked leaves,
their guarded Provençal secrecy
that only partly stills the force of their humming,
and looking out the window of
my dusty car, on the last part of the exercise
in mindfulness that is the road
into Tassajara, the hillside seemed
to leap toward me, close enough to touch,
and I saw that the dried creosote bushes
were purple in the midday light, and that
the hollows and the shadows in the hills
were the same blue green as in Monet's paintings
of the Valley of the Creuse, colors no one
had ever seen in hills and bushes until
he looked carefully and long
at those rough hills and their low,
clinging shrubs. I cross and recross the stream
on its rounded rocks, and pick my way
across a field of broken boulders. The rocks here
seem alive, set randomly, as they are,

by nature, or carefully by human hands to act
as markers, signs, tokens of place.
I miss Virginia, her red hair, her radiant smile,
her way of viewing life as if it were
a delightful toy, one that she knew she could make
even more amusing and more beautiful.
I thought that she would stay in my life, to teach me
how to love it, to show me how to grow old
without growing bitter, to see the world
as gift, not punishment.

I had forgotten how far this place was,
and when I finally reach the top of the path
that climbs along the side of a cliff,
only two people are at the Narrows,
standing naked on a curved shelf of granite.
The sun has left most of the ravine, and
I edge along the cliff downstream, past the chute
and the plunge to a place surrounded by young elms
and willows, where the sun still lies on
the huge stream-polished boulders.
I climb onto the largest one and take off my clothes
to lie here in the sun, the rock
as smooth and warm as human skin. It cradles me
like a hand, and I think that
I can hear it humming, the sound

of its molecules whirling in ecstasy,
holding me up on the moon-pale netted surface
of speckled pigment and shining crystals,
and I remember Jeffers's "Oh, Lovely Rock,"
written after camping on Ventana Creek,
where he talks about the passion and nobility
of rocks. The hillside rises
sharply beside me like high desert above this small
oasis: fractured iron-colored rock
and lichen-streaked and -mottled rock faces, gray-green
sword-leafed sunbursts of yucca.
You must all have been gazelles in the forest
of the Buddha, said the lecturer at Green Gulch,
speaking of our privileged, expensive lives
on this semi-arid land that grows ever more valuable,
Tor House, which once stood alone, now hard to find
among the million-dollar homes of Carmel Point.
Yes, we are lucky. The Indians who walked
hundreds of miles to these sulphur springs
have vanished. The cries of those who live their lives
in misery only faintly reach this place, while we
have too much of everything, except water. Now,
in the fourth year of drought
some of the trees are dying in the Santa Lucia,
and small, pinch-faced gray foxes
come in to Tassajara, looking for food.

Yet there is some strange kind of clarity here,
a cleanness in the fragrance of the sun-dried leaves,
the powdery yellow dust, a sense of matter
being grateful for its solidity and form,
and the rock pours from the ground in smooth,
silvery waves, folds and flows of granite
like a pouring out of grace from earth's deep heart,
the kind of free, unexpected giving that makes us know
that we, and everything we see, are holy.

Swimming

for Marilyn

My old friend and I step down into the pool's warm
chlorinated water, no longer thin, dark-haired girls
as when we met. We push out into the lap lanes
in our women's bodies. Her hair, once chestnut,
to her waist, is cropped, completely white; mine is mostly gray.
We have survived womanhood, the scars hidden
underneath our swimsuits: She has only one breast,
like an Amazon; I have empty space where my female organs were.
We swim slowly, inexpertly, without husbands or children,
as we were that summer night in Kansas City, with Ken and Bob
at the Jewel Box, our first female-impersonators' bar,
and the Blue Room, our first black bar, drinking
Singapore slings and sloe gin fizzes, staying up all night
and going swimming in our underwear at 4 A.M.
in a lake in Kansas. We built a fire on the shore,
and I told Bob he looked like Stephen Dedalus
in *Portrait of the Artist,* in the scene of his epiphany
on the beach. I've always liked to think I saved our lives
later, on the turnpike, by waking Ken when he dozed off
behind the wheel. Now, still young, he and Bob are dead of AIDS,
deaths none of us then could have imagined.

Old friends, we swim our slow, unathletic laps. We were
intense, emotional girls. We believed
that art made life worth living, and it does. We thought that life
would give us everything, and it has.
We are still burning, plunging through the pool's bright surface,
buoyant in the sweet and bitter water.

In the Arboretum

for Robert

Spring turns into summer; the planet has tilted over
as far as it will go, and we have as much light
as we will be allowed in this life, in this latitude.
Mars, Jupiter, and Venus are slow-dancing with the moon
low in the western sky; each night they change places, and
the moon surprises us with her new body.
Because it is near Midsummer's Eve, someone has built
a Celtic Burning Man on a barge out in the bay, where it glows
each night not with fire, but neon.
    Early on Sunday morning, I meet my friends
Jessie and Robert, who each live near the park
and often walk together in the arboretum.
She has brought bagels, cream cheese, fruit, and jam;
he has brought French roast in a thermos.
After eating breakfast on the grass, in the clear sunlight,
Robert and I take the picnic things back to the car. *I guess*
Jessie told you, he says, *that I tested HIV-positive.*
No, I say, *she didn't tell me,* as for a moment, the light falters.
He tells me that he is not afraid to die. I say,
They could find a cure. I say, *Anything can happen.*
We walk slowly back toward the arboretum,
and he and Jessie take me to the cool cloud forest,
where the plants feed on air. Then we walk
to the redwood grove, where the giant trees reach up to make
their own atmosphere, transpiring clouds of moisture over
their deep-green crowns. At their feet, a smaller, brighter forest
of new-green redwood shoots.

Strolling in sun, in shade, we feel cared for
in this place where everything is cared for.
Jessie and Robert tell me they never see the gardeners,
who work on weekdays, so that new trees and flowers
appear for them each weekend like magic.
From the moonscape of the cactus garden, we walk past
the chaparral, past the California native plants
and the lily ponds, where we discuss the differences between
irises and flags, to the moon-viewing platform where
we cannot see the moon, because it is shining down on China.
So we gaze across the water, death in all of us, but burning brighter,
closer to the surface in one, and they tell me how wonderful
it was here in winter, when the lakes were frozen in the record cold.
Despite the freeze and the drought and the lack of public funds,
the park is lush; the magnolias are about to bloom, and we find
several kinds of dogwood, and the last of the rhododendrons.
Jessie exclaims over the water lilies and the columbines. Now
she and Robert are pretending that this is their garden, and I am
their guest. I keep thinking of a Buddhist text: *There is an arrow*
in the heart of every flower, and it points at you.
Crossing the wide expanse of lawn, we walk through the last
special place, the fragrance garden, where we break off leaves
of daphne, thyme, oregano, five kinds of mint, scented geranium,
and crush them in our hands until the leaves turn bruised and dark.
We hold them to our faces, and breathe in.

Under the Magnolia

I give thanks because I do not have
a great sorrow. My village has not
burned, my child has not died, my body
is not ravaged. I sit here on the ground
lucky, lucky. Somewhere, villages are burning,
somewhere, not too far away, children
are dying; in this great urban park
painstakingly constructed over sand dunes,
people live in the flowering bushes. But
just here, in front of me, is a bride and groom;
here is a child running with
a red ball; another child is rolling on
the grass. All I have to do is to decide
how much fear to let inside my heart
in this fragile, created place, this bowl of grass
surrounded by palms and cypresses and
shaggy-barked cedars and trees
whose names I do not know, long fronds
falling, clusters of lilac fruits depending like
bouquets. All we can do is trust
that we belong here with the flowers: white
iris and Iceland poppies, a blur
of primroses, beds where flowers are
a crowd of color, where they close in the dark,
where the first light finds them starred
with dew. The trees seem to know

what I do not know; even the cultivated grass
understands some chain of being I can only
guess at, whether it is God's mind, or
the erotic body of the Goddess, or some
abstract kind of love, or
some longing for existence that includes
the fern trees, the new buds of cones on the
conifers, the white butterflies, the skating boys,
the hooked new buds of the magnolia
that look like claws holding on
to life, the curved thick petals of magnolia
in the grass, some gone to rust, some creased,
some streaked, others freckled, others magenta
at the curved stem end, others cracked,
all lined with long veins branching out
to the petal's edge.

The Road to Emmaus

All around us, secrets are continually
revealed. Even on some back road
in an abandoned country, far
from any trade route, a gravel road
where every passing car is showered
with yellow dust, and dust coats
the brush and milkweed and
black-eyed Susans crowding its edges,
anyone could be a shining stranger
in disguise, his raiment
dulled by dust, his feet stumbling
on the river pebbles. Patches of dock
and lamb's-quarter, stands of pokeweed,
the road crossing Bear Creek
five times on the way to the farm, hidden truths
and miracles in the heart of the flowers,
revelations among the minnows in
the shallow water the road dips into, the birds
trying and trying to tell us
the kingdom is here, on the earth.

At the End of October

for Nora

Here is the garden: the ridged, misshapen quinces,
glowing like lanterns, smelling of apples and roses;
the heavy pomegranates, hung on thin branches, spattered
with ruby, blood, fire, dried stamens clutched
in the blossom hole. The fig trees' spatulate leaves, ripe figs dark
against sheer, unending blue. Persimmons burning like
so many setting suns. The smoky ends of days, the tilted
light, odor of fallen leaves, that mix of honey and regret.
Far below, in the black kingdom of dirt and stone, the seed-daughter
pulls her robes close against the cold. Above us each night:
the swelling moon, the bright belt of the Hunter.

Elegy for a Poet

for Tom McAfee

I know you have no knowledge now that you are dead;
you don't come back, longing for the world. Yet I am heavier
than when you were alive, drinking yourself to death
back in Missouri. I carry you with me, wondering why you stayed
among the students, who grew younger every year. It makes me sad
to think of you going down to the river again and again,
the target practice and the beer, the sun on so many leaves.
But you stayed, in the Three Cheers Lounge, with the beer signs
blinking different colors. Outside: old wooden houses,
their porches spread like aprons, bordered by zinnias,
petunias, marigolds—all those reeking flowers—
and the thick air, like a hand across the face.
    Here, the trees are manageable, polite, except the eucalyptuses
growing out of control, sending medicinal fumes across the hills.
Back home, the trees stretch wider, higher than the houses:
universes shadowing the kitchens. Here, the streets rise and fall
and are bare, like the decks of ships. The wind blows
almost constantly, as if through rigging; low clouds rush by,
part of the voyage. Every street is lined with houses
whose windows are angled, faceted, like the eyes of bees. But Tom,
I have to tell you that these rooms with windowed bays
are shaped like coffins; their ceilings are exactly like
the ceilings of the dead.

Not long ago I drove up the coast; I thought of you. The hills
were green, and sprinkled with bird-shaped flowers. On Mount Tam
ferns sprang out of the earth like fountains; the wild white irises
looked like fallen stars. I can't remember ever
hearing so many birds. And everywhere—the smell of dust
and bitter herbs in the underbrush.

I just saw *Mr. Hulot's Holiday* again after all these years,
and when they boarded up the concession stands, and everyone
but Mr. Hulot left the beach, I thought of you, dying in August.
I remembered how you loved moments, but not life. I remembered
your pain and arrogance, your foolishness and grace.

Sometimes the days pour out like wine; though nothing
has turned out the way I thought, there is a sweetness to my life.
Above the surface of my skin is the girl you knew; just beneath I see
the old woman I will become. I no longer have that recurring dream
in which I come back to see you and you don't know who I am.
Somehow, now that you aren't in the world, you are part of me.
Your laughter has stopped; but in a way I don't quite understand,
my teacher, it is not lost.

He Glides Through the Streets of Paris, Surrounded by Clouds

Dali's lectures expounding his inexplicable "paranoiac-critical" method always drew crowds. For a lecture at the Sorbonne, he arrived in a white Rolls-Royce that was filled to the brim with cauliflower. . . .

—JAMES R. MELLOW,
New York Times Book Review

There is not enough white in the world, only
the Alps, blank canvases and sheets of paper,
melting eyeballs and watch faces, nightgowns
and bedsheets. So little white in Paris, just *crème fraîche*
and candles, pale French faces, the infrequent snows
I dance through, making a random pattern of dark smudges
in the courtyard of the Louvre, and the cold
white northern light that floods the bowl
the layered city lies in. Everyone knows
there are not enough gardenias or white camellias,
that the world is longing for armloads of lilies
and white roses. But here am I, dressed all in white—
my linen suit with the brocade vest, a starched
shirt and cravat, patent leather shoes and spats—
shining a stellar light on my frightening black eyes
and hair and mustache. A prince of art, I take my place
in the back of the splendid white machine, which Raffaello
then fills with innumerable rough hard clouds
of the white cauliflower, which give off a small
stink of cabbage and the rich manure of the market gardens
outside Paris, so many tight white heads of stopped,

incipient bloom jostling against me as Ángel drives me
through the cracked, encrusted streets, past buildings black
with coal dust, effortlessly and without sound
gliding through the narrow medieval byways, over
the buried limestone quarries and lost streams,
down the melancholy rue des Écoles to the gray building
where the public waits, where I, the artist,
will descend in a blinding avalanche of vegetables,
delivering a vision.

The Luncheon of the Boating Party

It would be impossible to find
the representation of something ugly
in any picture by [Renoir], anything
to suggest sadness or bitterness. . . .
neither his money worries nor his illness
left the slightest trace in his art.

—Pierre D'Espezel and François Fosca,
The Pageant of Painting

Midafternoon, toward the end of summer. The sun is warm
on the red-and-white-striped awning. Lunch has ended.
On the table, thick white rumpled linen is weighted down
with grapes, bottles of wine, half-filled fluted glasses
of pale wine, dark wine. Sun touches everything:
It lights the faces of the boating party, and light glows
from their faces, the women with their pink and white
apple blossom skin, the men more golden. One of the rowers,
leaning bare-armed on the rail, seems filled with sun,
red-gold hair springing from his head and chin
like the sun's corona. Everyone is at ease, content.
A man leans over the chair of the woman dressed in blue.
On her red, curling hair she wears a tilted hat
of pleated cloth, shaped like a small soufflé.
A woman lifts a wineglass to her lips; another rests, smiling,
on the rail. One woman wears a straw hat topped with flowers;
she is cooing to her tiny, bright-eyed dog. There must be
soft laughter, murmuring, the yipping of the dog,
the sound of awning fringe fluttering.

Light wind stirs the willows at the river's edge, green
edged with sun and blue with shadow; beyond the trees
small boats float on the water. There is no sorrow here,
no pain; we know that they exist only by their absence. Life
spills out of the painting into the room where it is hung:
The canvas, flat, rectangular, can't contain this long
golden afternoon. Against the ache and sorrow of the world
we lift our glasses: the color of sunlight,
the color of the heart.

Whorl

filament,
spume, spore,
volute,
protoplasm.
Jelly, seastack.
Seaweed
fans, feather
boas, alluvial plains,
sperm, green candy,
coral branches,
Christmas cactus.
The air mineral,
oxygen, crystal,
iodine, furred with salt
rime, reeking
of ocean, massed
with gnats
and sea flies. Pure
white sand, round pale
boulders, broken
edges of conglomerate
rock, beads of white and
ivory and pink, sea
glass, lost legs
of crabs. All

beating like a heart:
undulating
surface of the sea,
invisible
moon, curving
silver line of the horizon.
Water, cradle, blue
immensity.

Les Nymphéas

They were there from the beginning, just emerging
from the canvas in the shape of sunlight dappled
on the white skirt of a woman's dress, masses of color
in a garden, whorls of light on the face of the sea.
Finally, they took root in a stopped pool of the Epte and
blossomed into paintings, room after room of them suspended
on the walls, swimming in blue ponds, the green
circling, the sun-shot depths, floating on the glassy
surface, the river of reflected light, the shadow world
of leaves and lilies and river water,
anchored in mud, facing the sky,
clouds mirrored around them and the glowing,
partially divided lily pads.

Water lilies at dawn, just opening their spiked white
corolla, slowly revealing the rayed sun at their heart,
light intensifying around them. The creamy, sculpted petals
of water lilies at noon, when the sun has drawn
all color up into itself like the moon pulling the water
towards it; and in the afternoon, when,
the sun slanted down toward the horizon, the colors
deepen as the odors of flowers ripen
in those long, departing hours.

And water lilies at sunset, when the sun makes the water burn,
a river of fire leading into death. *This is a painting*
about death, I thought, the minute I saw it, how it is like
a welcoming warm avenue of color with light burning
beyond, how it enriches everything around it, how
the world glows with it, as if it too were on fire,
how we float, almost but not quite drowning, our lives
a reflection and a circling and a rootedness
in mud, balanced between the water and the sky,
how we will follow the dying sun across
water and the closing bodies of the lilies. Then the last
great painting, wide as eternity, with the white space
at the center, a paradise of color and emptiness and
indistinct flowers or the memory of flowers, or
the spirits of the flowers, and the enduring light,
and its reflection in the waters of the world.

Notes

This book is dedicated to Tom McAfee, my poetry teacher at the University of Missouri.

The title of “Simple Mysteries” is a phrase from a Russian poem, author unknown.

The poem “After Cocteau” is based on the first scene of Jean Cocteau’s 1946 film, *La Belle et la Bête*.

The first line of “Poem for My Childhood” is a paraphrase of a line from a poem by Duane BigEagle.

About the Author

Carolyn Miller is a book editor, writer, and painter living in San Francisco. *Constant Lover,* a letterpress limited-edition collection of her poems, was published by Protean Press in 2001. *The Reluctant Dinner Guest,* a chapbook, was included in *A Small Box of Poets,* also by Protean Press. Her poetry has received the James Boatwright III Award for Poetry from *Shenandoah* and the Rainmaker Award from *Zone 3*. She leads writing workshops in San Francisco and at La Serranía, a retreat center on the island of Mallorca.

Sixteen Rivers Press is a shared-work, not-for-profit poetry collective dedicated to providing an alternative publishing avenue for San Francisco Bay Area poets. Founded in 1999 by seven women writers, the press is named for the sixteen rivers that flow into San Francisco Bay.

SAN JOAQUIN • FRESNO • CHOWCHILLA • MERCED • TUOLUMNE • STANISLAUS
CALAVERAS • BEAR • MOKELUMNE • COSUMNES • AMERICAN • YUBA • FEATHER
SACRAMENTO • NAPA • PETALUMA

Design: Carolyn Miller

Text: Times

Display: Walters and Brice

Printer and binder: McNaughton & Gunn